SCHOLASTIC

News

Nonfiction Readers

Comets

by
Melanie Chrismer

Children's Press
An Imprint of Scholastic Inc.
New York Toronto London Auckland Sydney
Mexico City New Delhi Hong Kong
Danbury, Connecticut

These content vocabulary word builders
are for grades 1–2.

Consultant: Michelle Yehling, Astronomy Education Consultant

Photo Credits:

Photographs © 2008: Corbis Images/Ali Jarekji/Reuters: 17; Getty Images: 5 bottom left, 15 (Digital Vision), 4 bottom left, 9 (Francesco Reginato/The Image Bank); Photo Researchers, NY: 5 top right (Chris Butler), 4 top, 20 bottom, 21 bottom, 21 top, 23 (John Chumack), 4 bottom right, 13 (Mark Garlick), 11 (Pekka Parviainen), 2, 5 bottom right, 20 top, 23 spot art (Kitt Peak/Aura), 19 (Rev. Ronald Royer), cover, 1, 5 top left, 7 (Frank Zullo); PhotoDisc/Getty Images via SODA: back cover.

Book Design: Simonsays Design!
Book Production: The Design Lab

Library of Congress Cataloging-in-Publication Data
Chrismer, Melanie.
Comets / by Melanie Chrismer.—Updated ed.
     p. cm.—(Scholastic news nonfiction readers)
Includes bibliographical references and index.
ISBN-13: 978-0-531-14694-1 (lib. bdg.)   978-0-531-14759-7 (pbk.)
ISBN-10: 0-531-14694-4 (lib. bdg.)   0-531-14759-2 (pbk.)
1. Comets—Juvenile literature. I. Title.
QB721.5.C57   2007
523.6—dc22   2006102766

17 18 19 20 21 R 23 22 21

Scholastic Inc., 557 Broadway, New York, NY 10012.

CONTENTS

WORD HUNT

Look for these words as you read. They will be in **bold**.

coma
(**koh**-muh)

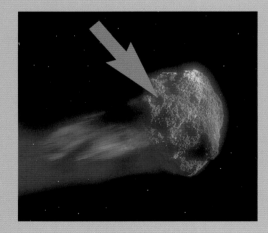

nucleus
(**noo**-klee-uhss)

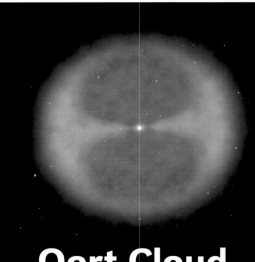

Oort Cloud
(ort kloud)

4

comet
(**kom**-it)

Kuiper Belt
(**ki**-per belt)

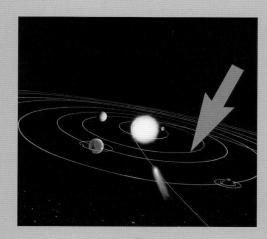

orbit
(**or**-bit)

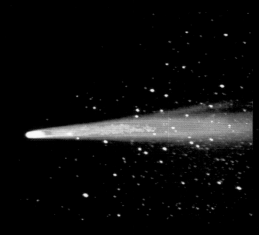

outer space
(**ou**-tur spayss)

5

Comets!

Can you catch a **comet** by one of its tails?

No. One tail is made of dust. The other tail is made of gas.

There is nothing to hold onto.

dust

gas

7

A comet is a big chunk of frozen water and gases with dust.

When a comet gets close to the Sun, it changes.

The Sun heats up the comet.

Most of the center, or **nucleus,** of the comet stays frozen.

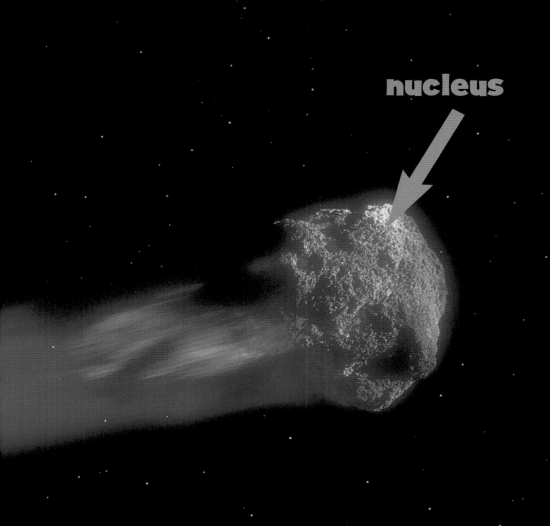

nucleus

The surface of the comet starts to come apart.

This makes a cloud around the nucleus called a **coma**.

Two tails are formed.

One tail is dust coming off the comet.

The other tail is made of gas.

This comet is heating up.

gas tail

dust tail

Scientists think comets come from the **Kuiper Belt** or the **Oort Cloud**.

The Kuiper Belt begins near the planet Neptune.

The Oort Cloud is very far out in space.

Scientists think the Oort Cloud surrounds the solar system.

Most comets travel around the Sun on a path called an **orbit**.

We do not see them all the time.

The orbits of many comets take them very far away in **outer space**.

Some do not come back for a long time.

Sun

comet

Some comets leave pieces of dust and rock behind.

When Earth passes through the path of comet pieces, they burn up.

They make streaks of light called meteors or shooting stars.

Sometimes we see many meteors at the same time. This is called a meteor shower.

A good time to see meteors, or shooting stars, is in August.

Stay awake and keep your eyes on the sky.

Then, make a wish on a shooting star!

19

Famous Comets!

What is the most famous comet? Halley's comet!
It was last near Earth in 1986.
We won't see it again until the year 2061.

Did you see comet NEAT?
It was here in May 2004.

Look! It's comet Hale-Bopp.
Look at it glow.
It was discovered in 1995.

This is comet Hyakutake.
Scientists think that comet Hyakutake
traveled around the Sun several thousand years ago.

YOUR NEW WORDS

coma (**koh**-muh) a glowing cloud of gas and dust around a comet

comet (**kom**-it) a big dusty chunk of ice that travels around the Sun in a long slow path

Kuiper Belt (**ki**-per belt) an area past Neptune where many icy objects orbit the Sun

nucleus (**noo**-klee-uhss) the center of a comet

Oort Cloud (ort kloud) an area very far past Pluto where scientists believe there are many comets

orbit (**or**-bit) the path an object takes around another object

outer space (**ou**-tur spayss) everything past the planet Earth and its atmosphere

Comets Are Amazing!

The word *comet* comes from the Greek word *kometes*. This means "very long hair".

When a comet heats up, part of it stays frozen and part does not.

A comet's tail can be millions of miles long.

Comets are big dusty chunks of ice.

Comets have four parts: a nucleus, a coma, and two tails.

INDEX

FIND OUT MORE

Book:

Kippes, Steven N. *Killer Rocks from Outer Space: Asteroids, Comets, and Meteors*. Minneapolis, MN: Lerner Publishing Group, 2004.

Web site:

Comet Information and Pictures
http://starchild.gsfc.nasa.gov/docs/StarChild/solar_system_level1/comets.html

MEET THE AUTHOR

Melanie Chrismer grew up near NASA in Houston, Texas. She loves math and science and has written thirteen books for children. To write her books, she visited NASA where she floated in the zero-gravity trainer called the Vomit Comet. She says, "it is the best roller coaster ever!"